MAYA
ANGELOU

POET, PERFORMER, ACTIVIST

SPECIAL LIVES IN HISTORY THAT BECOME

Signature LIVES

MAYA
·············
ANGELOU

POET, PERFORMER, ACTIVIST

by Don Nardo

Content Adviser: Carolyn J. Medine, Ph.D.,
Associate Professor, Institute for
African American Studies and Institute for
Women's Studies, University of Georgia

Reading Adviser: Alexa L. Sandmann, Ed.D.,
Professor of Literacy, College and Graduate School
of Education, Health and Human Services
Kent State University

Compass Point Books ✦ Minneapolis, Minnesota

Compass Point Books
151 Good Counsel Drive
P.O. Box 669
Mankato, MN 56002-0669

Editor: Jennifer VanVoorst
Page Production: Bobbie Nuytten
Photo Researcher: Svetlana Zhurkin
Cartographer: XNR Productions, Inc.
Library Consultant: Kathleen Baxter

Art Director: LuAnn Ascheman-Adams
Creative Director: Joe Ewest
Editorial Director: Nick Healy
Managing Editor: Catherine Neitge

Library of Congress Cataloging-in-Publication Data
Nardo, Don, 1947–
   Maya Angelou : poet, performer, activist / by Don Nardo.
      p. cm. — (Signature Lives)
   Includes bibliographical references and index.
   ISBN 978-0-7565-1889-9 (library binding)
1. Angelou, Maya—Juvenile literature. 2. Authors, American—20th
century—Biography—Juvenile literature. 3. Women authors,
American—Biography—Juvenile literature. 4. African American authors—
Biography—Juvenile literature. 5. African American women civil rights
workers—Biography—Juvenile literature. I. Title. II. Series.
   PS3551.N464Z7975 2009
   818'.5409—dc22
   [B]   2008041488

Visit Compass Point Books on the Internet at *www.compasspointbooks.com*
or e-mail your request to *custserv@compasspointbooks.com*

MODERN AMERICA

Life in the United States since the late 19th century has undergone incredible changes. Advancements in technology and in society itself have transformed the lives of Americans. As they adjusted to this modern era, people cast aside old ways and embraced new ideas. The once silenced members of society—women, minorities, and young people—made their voices heard. Modern Americans survived wars, economic depression, protests, and scandals to emerge strong and ready to face whatever the future holds.

Table of Contents

1 "On the Pulse of Morning"

~~~ε·∽~~~

On January 20, 1993, 64-year-old Maya Angelou stood before the tens of thousands of people who had gathered at the U.S. Capitol in Washington, D.C. They were there to witness the inauguration of Bill Clinton as 42nd president of the United States. This was only the second time in history that a poet had been chosen to recite at a presidential inauguration. It was a historic occasion, and Angelou was nervous. "I tried not to realize where I was," she later said. "I tried to suspend myself. I was afraid I might lose my composure."

Angelou had worked for weeks on the poem. She thought about the complicated history of her people and her country, and she thought about the future. She filled up five pads of paper with ideas and phrases.

Maya Angelou presented her poem "On the Pulse of Morning" to thousands of onlookers and millions of TV viewers on January 20, 1993.

> *The first poet to speak at a presidential inauguration was Robert Frost, who read his poem "The Gift Outright" at the inauguration of President John F. Kennedy in 1961.*

Eventually her ideas took shape. "On the Pulse of Morning," the poem she created for the occasion, is full of grace and hope. It speaks of the dignity of all people and calls for peace, justice, and healing. So on that cold January day, despite her nerves, Maya Angelou had an important message to deliver. With great poise and emotion, and in her rich, ringing voice, she read:

History, despite its wrenching pain,
Cannot be unlived, and if faced with courage,
Need not be lived again.
Lift up your eyes upon
The day breaking for you.
Give birth again
To the dream.
Women, children, men,
Take it into the palms of your hands.
Mold it into the shape of your most
Private need. Sculpt it into
The image of your most public self.
Lift up your hearts.
Each new hour holds new chances
For new beginnings.
...
Here on the pulse of this new day
You may have the grace to look up and out
And into your sister's eyes,
Into your brother's face, your country

And say simply
Very simply
With hope
Good morning.

Angelou has had a close relationship with President Bill Clinton; in 2000, he presented her with the National Medal of Arts for her contributions to American literature.

Angelou considers her role in the inauguration to be her most noteworthy achievement. But even before her history-making performance, she had already made many great—even history-making—achievements in a wide range of professions. She was the first African-American streetcar conductor in San Francisco. She toured the world as a performing artist and acted in a popular television miniseries. She worked in the civil rights movement. And when she finally turned her hand to writing, she became the

Maya Angelou has made history through her achievements in a wide variety of professions.

first African-American to win the National Book Award for her autobiography *I Know Why the Caged Bird Sings.* Her six autobiographical novels and many collections of poems examine the African-American experience as well as the human experience in language that is both rich and straightforward. Her unofficial title of "people's poet" is well-earned.

Over the course of her long and varied career, Maya Angelou has become an influential and beloved figure in American culture. Her writings, speeches, and performances remind us of the bond all human beings share. Her remarkable life encourages us all to overcome obstacles and live to our full potential.

Maya Angelou has earned the unofficial title of "people's poet" through her inspiring, accessible poetry and the many public events where she has presented it. In addition to speaking at President Clinton's inauguration, Angelou delivered another poem, "A Brave and Startling Truth," in 1995 at the 50th anniversary of the founding of the United Nations. And in October of that year, she read "From a Black Woman to a Black Man" at the Million Man March in Washington, D.C.

2 A HECTIC AND SCARY CHILDHOOD

∽⟨×⟩∾

The woman the world would later come to know as Maya Angelou was born Marguerite Annie Johnson in the bustling city of St. Louis, Missouri. The date was April 4, 1928. Her father, Bailey Johnson, worked as a doorman and dietician. Her mother, Vivian Baxter Johnson, was a nurse. She also dealt cards in a gambling casino. The new baby had a brother, Bailey Junior, who was a year older than she. When he started talking, he had trouble pronouncing his sister's name, so he called her "Mya sister." In time, it became simply Maya. The Johnsons thought this was cute, so they called her Maya, too, and the name stuck.

Not long after Maya was born, her parents moved the family to Long Beach, California. Their marriage

---

African-Americans were second-class citizens in the segregated South; even drinking fountains were marked "Colored."

was not happy, however. Soon after arriving in Long Beach, the couple decided to get divorced. Bailey Senior stayed in California, and Vivian headed back to St. Louis.

Their father took Maya and Bailey Junior to the local train station. He tied little cards around their wrists. The cards read "To Whom It May Concern," followed by the children's names and the place they were traveling to. Then he shipped them by train to that destination— the small, rural town of Stamps, Arkansas. They were going there to live with their grandmother, Annie Henderson Johnson, Bailey Senior's mother. Her son Willie, the children's uncle, lived there, too. Maya later recalled:

When Maya Angelou grew up, she learned that the trip she and her brother had made across the country alone was not unusual. In her first autobiography, I Know Why the Caged Bird Sings, she wrote: "Years later I discovered that the United States had been crossed thousands of times by frightened Black children traveling alone to their newly affluent parents in Northern cities, or back to grandmothers in Southern towns when the urban North reneged on [went back on] its economic promises."

> *I don't remember much of the trip. But after we reached the segregated southern part of the journey, things must have looked up. Negro passengers, who always traveled with loaded lunch boxes, felt sorry for "the poor little motherless darlings" and plied us with cold fried chicken and potato salad.*

Arriving in Stamps, Maya found that her grandmother owned and ran a small general store in the African-American section of town. Annie and her son Willie lived in a couple of small rooms at the back of the store. Three-year-old Maya and 4-year-old Bailey Junior moved in with them. Maya came to care deeply for her grandmother and often called her Momma. Annie Henderson did her best to raise the children. She took them to the local black Methodist church every Sunday. And as they grew older and stronger, she gave them little jobs to do in the family store. Maya, for example, poured flour, sugar, and corn into paper bags for the customers.

Actors playing Maya and her grandmother stood in the store in a scene from the movie version of Angelou's autobiography I Know Why the Caged Bird Sings.

At the time Maya Angelou was born, racism, discrimination, and unfair treatment of African-Americans was still the norm in the United States. It was particularly prevalent in the South. There whites and blacks shared an uneasy coexistence. African-Americans were second-class citizens who could not shop at white-owned stores or eat in white restaurants. Blacks also made less money than whites for doing the same work. In the 1930s, for example, Southern black farmers made about $200 per year. In comparison, white farmers averaged from $600 to $1,000 per year. In the same period, 50 percent of blacks were unemployed, while white unemployment was 25 percent.

Part of the children's new upbringing consisted of learning the stark facts of Southern life for African-Americans. Their grandmother explained that Stamps and other Southern towns were strictly segregated. That meant that whites and blacks lived apart. Moreover, white people held all the well-paying jobs and positions of power and influence. And if a black person did something that angered or threatened a white person, the black person could be brutalized, or even killed. For that reason, Maya's grandmother warned her not to trust "white folks." In fact, Annie said, it was better for the children to avoid even talking to them.

The result was that young Maya long believed white people should be distrusted and feared. She later remembered:

> In Stamps, the segregation was so complete that most Black children didn't really, absolutely know what whites looked like. Other than that they were

different, to be dreaded, and in that dread was included the hostility of the powerless against the powerful, the poor against the rich, the worker against the worked for, and the ragged against the well dressed.

Another belief that young Maya held for several years was that her parents were both dead. Why else, she wondered, had she and her brother ended up in Arkansas with their grandmother? "I could cry anytime I wanted," she later wrote, "by picturing my mother ... lying in her coffin. Her hair, which was black, was spread out on a tiny little white pillow and

As a child, Maya traveled around the country, living with relatives in the Midwest, South, and West.

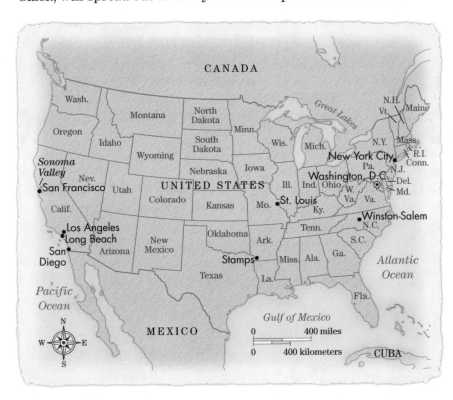

her body was covered with a sheet."

Maya's parents were still very much alive, however, as she discovered when she was 6. Christmas gifts arrived for her and Bailey Junior from both their parents. Maya received a doll and a toy tea set from her mother, and her father sent a photograph of himself. But instead of being pleased by the gifts—and the realization that her parents were alive—Maya went outside and cried. She wondered if her parents had sent her away because she had done something wrong.

The following year, when Maya was 7, her father arrived at her grandmother's store. He said he had come to take Maya and Bailey Junior to live with their mother in St. Louis. This was quite unexpected. Maya was afraid that the woman who had sent her away years before might not like her.

Fortunately for Maya, Vivian Johnson loved her daughter dearly. She had also missed her a great deal. Maya instantly felt a powerful connection with and attraction for her mother, and she later said:

> To describe my mother would be to write about a hurricane in its perfect power. Or the climbing, falling colors of a rainbow. … It is remarkable how much truth there is in the two expressions "struck dumb" and "love at first sight." … I knew immediately why she had sent me away. She was too beautiful to have children.

As an adult, Angelou's relationship with her mother strengthened.

That was not the real reason that Vivian had lived apart from her children for four years, of course. She had lacked the means of supporting them after separating from her husband. But now she was able to give Maya her own room. The young girl also had a radio and store-bought clothes for the first time.

Though Maya found much to be happy about in her new home, she soon found that there was a dark side, too. Her mother's boyfriend, whom Maya knew as Mr. Freeman, lived in the same house. One day when her mother was out, Freeman raped Maya in the living room. When Maya's mother and uncles found out what had happened, they had Freeman arrested. Maya testified at his trial, and the jury

A young actor playing Maya took the stand to testify in a scene from the movie I Know Why the Caged Bird Sings.

sentenced him to a year and a day in prison. His lawyer, however, managed to get him released for that afternoon. That very day, he was kicked to death and his body dumped behind a slaughterhouse. Some people suspected that Maya's uncles had done the deed, but no charges were ever brought.

At the tender age of 7, Maya had been forced to deal with both violence and death on a very personal level. She had no way of knowing that other unsavory experiences awaited her. Her long road to literary greatness was destined to be a bumpy one. ◈

3 Chapter

HOOKED ON BOOKS

⤜⤛⤚

After Maya's rape, the trial of her attacker, and his murder, her mother sent her and her brother back to her grandmother in Stamps. At the time, the 8-year-old girl did not understand why she was leaving her mother again. She did not know that her relatives had agreed it would better for her to get away from the scene of her trauma for a while. In fact, Maya did not object to the move. She felt safe in Stamps with her grandmother and Uncle Willie.

Annie and Willie noticed a major difference in Maya this time, however. Put simply, the girl refused to speak. Not a single word issued from her lips from the time she woke up until the time she went to bed. Her family assumed her silence was a reaction to the violent attack she had suffered. What they did not

Actors Constance Good and John Driver played Maya and Bailey in the motion picture production of I Know Why the Caged Bird Sings.

know was that Maya was holding her tongue out of guilt. She believed that Freeman's brutal death had been her fault, and it would be better for her to stop talking so that she would not harm anyone else. "[I]f I talked to anyone else," she later recalled, "that person might die too. Just my breath, carrying my words out, might poison people and they'd curl up and die."

Maya remained mute for five years. She finally

started talking again, in large part because of the efforts of Bertha Flowers. A friend of Maya's grandmother, Flowers visited Annie at the store from time to time. Like other black people in town, Maya liked Bertha Flowers because she was kind, polite, and intelligent.

Flowers had heard about Maya's refusal to speak—even in school—and she wanted to try to help. She took the little girl aside and gently told her, "Now, no one is going to make you talk—possibly no one can. But bear in mind, language is man's way of communicating with his fellow man and it is language alone which separates him from the lower animals." Maya was intrigued by this idea, which was totally new to her. Flowers added, "Words mean more than what is set down on paper. It takes the human voice to infuse [fill] them with the shades of deeper meaning."

Maya spent many afternoons at Flowers' house. The older woman read to her from a variety of books. One that Maya later remembered

Bertha Flowers introduced Maya to books and learning, but she also taught the young girl that there was another important kind of knowledge that should be respected. This was common sense, which, she said, some people who lack formal education have. In her first autobiography, Maya remembered: "She [Flowers] said that ... some people, unable to go to school, were more educated and even more intelligent than college professors. She encouraged me to listen carefully to what country people called mother wit. That in those homely sayings was couched the collective wisdom of generations."

fondly was Charles Dickens' classic story of heroism during the French Revolution, _A Tale of Two Cities_. As Maya listened to Flowers' musical-sounding voice, she became entranced. Whatever the older woman read sounded like poetry. Maya longed to be able to recite words that easily and beautifully.

In this way, Maya slowly came out of her shell and began to speak again. Often she took a book Flowers had loaned her to a corner of the store and read out loud, quietly but intently. Customers found that they had to tap on the counter to get her attention.

Langston Hughes (1902–1967)

When Maya was 12, Flowers took her to the school library. She advised the girl to begin reading. Start with books having titles that begin with the letter _A_, she said, and keep going right through the alphabet. Maya eagerly followed this advice. She eventually read every book in the library. Among the works she absorbed were some by black writers such as Langston Hughes, Paul Laurence Dunbar, and James Weldon

Johnson. Johnson was one of Maya's favorite writers. In 1900, he wrote the lyrics for the song "Lift Every Voice and Sing," which is sometimes called the African-American national anthem. Maya also read works by great white writers, including William Shakespeare and Edgar Allan Poe. As an adult, Maya realized that these readings had been an education in themselves. They were the foundation on which she would steadily fashion an extraordinary ability to express herself through writing.

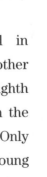

James Weldon Johnson (1871–1938)

Maya graduated from grammar school in 1940, when she was 12. In Stamps and many other Southern towns, grammar school ended in the eighth grade. Also, for most Southern black children the eighth grade marked the end of their education. Only a handful of very bright—or very fortunate—young African-Americans went on to higher education. Maya was one of them.

However, both her grandmother and her parents felt that Maya could not get a good education in the South. They decided to send her, along with her brother, to live with their mother again. By this time, her mother was living in California. Maya and her brother moved there when they were 13 and 14, respectively.

Not long after the children arrived in their new home, their mother married a mild-mannered man whom Maya called Daddy Clidell. He moved the family to San Francisco, where Maya enrolled in George Washington High School. For a while, she felt awkward in school. This was partly because she was one of only three African-American students in the mostly white school. Also, she was very tall for her age—5 feet 9 inches (175 centimeters). She later recalled that she felt like a horse.

Maya felt much more at ease in evening dance classes she began attending when she was 14. She later recalled:

> *My shyness at moving clad in black tights around a large empty room did not last long. Of course, at first, I thought everyone would be staring at my cucumber-shaped body with its knobs for knees, knobs for elbow, and, alas, knobs for breasts. But they really did not notice me, and when the teacher floated across the floor and finished in an arabesque [a graceful ballet move], my fancy was taken. I would learn to move like that.*

George Washington High School

In the summer of 1943, when Maya was 15, she traveled south to San Diego to spend some time with her father. Bailey Senior was living in a trailer park with his new girlfriend, Dolores Stockland. Maya and Dolores did not get along very well. Dolores was hoping to marry Bailey and was jealous of the time he spent with his daughter.

Maya attended San Francisco's George Washington High School, which was located in a white residential part of town.

The tense relationship came to a head after Bailey took Maya on a brief trip across the border into Mexico. As soon as they returned, Dolores and Bailey got into a loud argument. Bailey stormed out and went to a neighbor's house. Maya tried to comfort Dolores, but the older woman told her, "Why don't you go back to your mother? If you've got one." Maya later described the fight that followed:

The harbor city of San Diego, where Maya lived with her father, is located less than 20 miles (32 kilometers) from the Mexican border.

> *I walked to Dolores, enraged. ... "I'm going to slap you for that." ... I warned her and I*

slapped her. She was out of the chair like a flea, and before I could jump back, she had her arms around me. ... I had to push her shoulders with all my strength to unlock the octopus hold. Neither of us made a sound until I finally shoved her back onto the sofa. Then she started screaming. ... I walked out of the house. On the steps, I felt something wet on my arm and looked down to find blood.

Maya's father heard the commotion and came to the rescue. He saw that she had been stabbed, and he made sure that her cuts, which were minor, were treated. Then he dropped her off at a friend's house to keep her away from Dolores. Her father did not expect that Maya would run away and start living on the streets, but that is exactly what the headstrong, distressed, and confused young woman did. 𝔈𝔰

4 Chapter

TRIALS OF A YOUNG MOTHER

⁕⁒⁖⁒⁕

Maya was upset over her fight with Dolores. On impulse, she decided to run away. She later recalled that when she left she was carrying a few tuna sandwiches, some Band-Aids, and a little more than $3.

That evening, Maya came upon an old junkyard where people dumped their broken-down cars. She found that a group of teenagers—all runaways like herself—were living in the abandoned cars. Some did odd jobs during the day to make money to buy food. Others entered dance contests on weekends hoping to earn the prize money. Maya joined their group. The members were of all races, and over time, she grew more tolerant of people who were different from her. She later recalled:

*Odd that the homeless children ... could
initiate me into the brotherhood of man.
After hunting down unbroken bottles
and selling them with a white girl from
Missouri, a Mexican girl from Los Angeles
and a Black girl from Oklahoma, I was
never again to sense myself so solidly
outside the pale of the human race. The
lack of criticism evidenced by our ... community influenced me, and set a tone of
tolerance for my life.*

Though Maya gained some important insights from her new companions in San Diego, after a month she was homesick. She called her mother, who sent her a plane ticket back to San Francisco. Maya decided that instead of returning to school, her best course was to get a job and start saving some money for her future, whatever it might have in store. The profession of streetcar conductor appealed to her. "[T]he thought of sailing up and down the hills of San Francisco in a dark-blue uniform, with a money changer at my belt, caught my fancy," she later wrote.

The young woman was upset, therefore, when she learned that the streetcar company did not hire "colored people." Her mother, however, encouraged her to pursue her goal. "That's what you want to do?" she asked. "Then nothing beats a trial but a failure. Give it everything you've got."

Maya took this advice to heart. As expected, the streetcar company at first rejected her. But she kept showing up at the main office and urging those in charge to give her a chance. They finally gave in. At age 15, she became San Francisco's first African-American streetcar conductor. Soon she was proud to be "swinging on the back of the rackety trolley, smiling sweetly and persuading my charges [customers] to 'step forward in the car, please.'" But Maya's hunger for knowledge was too strong to be denied, and she

Cable cars began operating in San Francisco in 1873; they are still in use today.

returned to school after missing just one semester.

Although Maya's experiences sometimes made her seem more mature than her classmates, she was still a young woman, and she struggled with all the usual problems. For example, her body was beginning to change, and she felt uncomfortable in her own skin. "I noticed how heavy my own voice had become," she later remembered. "My hands and feet were also far from being feminine and dainty. ... For a sixteen-year-old, my breasts were sadly undeveloped." Eventually the young woman decided that she needed to get a boyfriend. She said, "A boyfriend would clarify my position to the world and, even more important, to myself."

The problem was that Maya was very naive in the area of male-female relationships. She went about getting a boyfriend in the wrong way. She simply went to a popular young man who lived in her neighborhood and asked him if he wanted to have sex. He said yes. Soon Maya found that she was pregnant.

The realization that she was going to have a baby marked a major turning point in Maya's life. At first, she was consumed with fear. She said:

> *The world had ended, and I was the only person who knew it. ... I alone was suffocating in the nightmare. The little pleasure I was able to take from the fact that ... I could have a baby ... was crowded*

into my mind's tiniest corner by the massive pushing in of fear, guilt and self-revulsion. For eons [ages], it seemed, I had accepted my plight as the hapless, put-upon victim of fate, ... but this time I had to face the fact that I had brought my new catastrophe upon myself.

Soon, however, these fears receded and were replaced by a sense of responsibility. Maya accepted the consequences of her mistake and vowed to do what was right for the child she was carrying. "I hefted the burden of pregnancy at sixteen onto my own shoulders where it belonged," she later wrote. "Admittedly, I staggered under the weight."

In July 1945, just weeks after graduating from San Francisco's Mission High School, Maya gave birth to a son, whom she named Clyde. World War II had just ended in Europe and would soon end in Asia. Tens of thousands of American men were returning to jobs that had been filled by women during the war years. This did not bode well for Maya. She had already quit her

In the 1940s, when Maya became pregnant, teen pregnancy was largely a taboo subject. Little accurate data for teenage pregnancy rates from that era exist. Today information about teenage pregnancy is more available and reliable. The National Campaign to Prevent Teen Pregnancy estimates that roughly 1 million teenage girls become pregnant each year in the United States. Less than one-third of teens who have babies before the age of 18 go on to finish high school.

job on the trolleys. And as a young woman with a child to support, she needed to find another job. She was turned down when she applied for a position as a telephone operator. But she managed to find work as a cook in a restaurant. After a relationship with a co-worker there ended in heartbreak, Maya decided she needed a change of scenery. She moved with baby Clyde to Los Angeles, where she found a job as a cocktail waitress at a nightclub called the Hi Hat Club.

Nightclubs in the 1940s often featured live entertainment such as singing, dancing, and theatrical performances.

Unfortunately for Maya, a number of shady people frequented the nightclub where she worked. Among them were thieves, con men, and prostitutes. Maya began making extra money by finding customers for two of the prostitutes. Eventually she had enough money to buy a new car. But then she and the two women got into an argument, and one of them threatened to tell the police what Maya had been doing.

Fearing what might happen to her child if she was arrested, Maya decided to take Clyde to Stamps. Her grandmother Annie welcomed them. But Maya was not destined to find security and happiness in the familiar surroundings of her youth. Soon the ugly face of racism would reappear and send her running once again. 🐱

5 A CAREER IN SHOW BUSINESS

❦

Back in Stamps, Maya found that she no longer fit in. Black people avoided the white sections of town. They also carefully avoided confrontations with white people, which could lead to anti-black violence. But her time in California had made Maya less afraid of white people. That was bound to get her into trouble in a Southern town.

One day Maya dressed in her nicest clothes and went to a store in the white part of town. There she got into a verbal tussle with two older white women. After accidentally bumping into a white female customer, the customer and the clerk demanded to know who Maya was. In a defiant voice, she replied that she was "Miss Johnson," and then added:

In 1957, Maya Angelou posed for a portrait in the dress she would wear in that year's Caribbean Calypso Festival.

I advise you to address me as Miss Johnson. For if I need to allude to your pitiful selves, I shall call you Miss Idiot, Miss Stupid, Miss Fool, or whatever name a luckless fate has dumped upon you. ... And where I'm from is no concern of yours, but rather where you're going. I'll slap you into the middle of next week if you even dare to open your mouths again.

By the time Maya got back home, her grandmother had already heard what had happened, and she was very angry. "You think 'cause you've been to California these crazy people won't kill you?" she asked Maya. In a reference to the Ku Klux Klan, a noted racist group, she added, "You think because of your all-fired principle some of the men won't feel like putting their white sheets on and riding over here to stir up trouble?"

It quickly became clear that Annie was right. Maya had gotten herself into a potentially dangerous situation. So she packed her and Clyde's things and returned to San Francisco.

Once more, Maya, now almost 19, began looking for a job. This time she seriously considered joining the U.S. Army. That way she could learn a trade and later get some money (through the G.I. Bill) to go to college. Her mother and other relatives were against the idea, but Maya's mind was made up. "Now I was ready," she later recalled. "Things had arranged them-

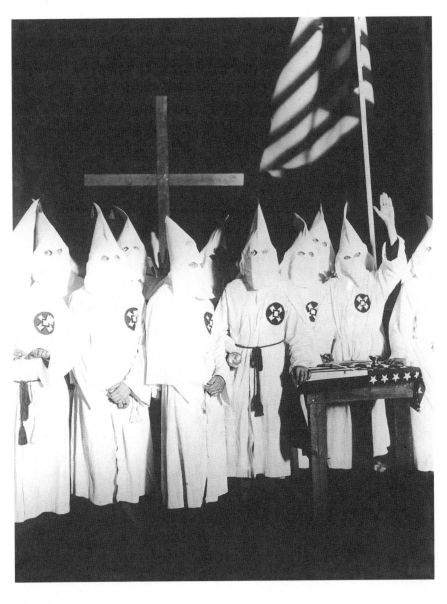

selves in my favor at last. For the next two years I would have the security of purpose and the dignity of being a soldier."

Members of the Ku Klux Klan terrorized blacks throughout the South.

Things did not go as Maya planned, however. She passed the physical, but the Army rejected her because they viewed the organization that ran the California dance school she had attended as a communist group.

Maya was naturally disappointed. But as it turned out, dancing—the supposed cause of her rejection—now came to her rescue. One of her friends happened to know a Chicago dancer named R.L. Poole. He was looking for a dancing partner, and she auditioned for him. Poole hired her. For a while they danced in a series of San Francisco nightclubs. She loved it. "I was a hungry person invited to a welcome table for the first time in her life," she later wrote. "I had broken in. I was in show business. The only way was up."

This turned out to be a bit of wishful thinking, however. After a while, Poole's old dancing partner returned, and Maya lost her job. After that, she began working as a fry cook in a little restaurant in nearby Stockton. There she met a man named L.D. Tolbrook, who was

Maya also performed with famed dancer and choreographer Alvin Ailey. The two met while attending modern dance classes in San Francisco and soon formed a successful but short-lived dance team they called Al and Rita. (Rita was a shortened form of her given name, Marguerite.) Ailey went on to form the renowned Alvin Ailey American Dance Theater, which brings African-American cultural expression and the American modern dance tradition to the world's stages.

her father's age. A smooth talker, he seduced her. He also told her that he badly needed money to pay some debts and convinced her to become a prostitute to earn the money. Because she thought she was in love

Maya performed an original African number at a California nightclub in the 1950s.

with him—and also because she was gullible—she agreed. While she was working, she left 3-year-old Clyde with a babysitter known as Big Mary.

About a month later, Maya's brother, Bailey Junior, found out what was happening. He warned his sister that Tolbrook was a con man and urged her to get Clyde and leave. She took her brother's advice. When she went to pick up Clyde, however, she found that Big Mary had left town and taken the boy with her. Maya soon caught up to Big Mary. The distraught and angry mother put Clyde in her car and drove back to San Francisco.

Maya's bad luck with men continued after she returned to her mother's place in San Francisco. The young woman found a job as a clerk in a record store. One day a white sailor entered the store, and he and Maya hit it off. His name was Tosh Angelos. When he later proposed marriage, she saw a chance for happiness and security and said yes. They were married in 1950 and moved into a large, rented apartment. But though Tosh was a kind man, the two had less in common than they had thought. They were divorced a little more than two years later.

A few months after her divorce, Maya, now 24, found a job as a dancer in a seedy nightclub, the Garden of Allah. It paid $75 a week. This was a low salary considering that she had to do six shows each night. Two months after taking the job, however, a performer at a high-class nightclub, the Purple Onion, saw her act and offered her a six-month contract. She accepted and began dancing there. She also performed as a calypso singer. Though her voice was untrained, her expressive delivery made the music come to life. Maya was a hit. Friends suggested that she needed a stage name to go with her new stage persona. She decided to keep Maya as a first name and changed the "s" in her ex-husband's name, Angelos, to a "u." In this way, she became Maya Angelou.

The newly named Maya Angelou struck a dramatic pose for a 1950s promotional photo.

*The cast of
Porgy and Bess
performed at
the Theatre de
l'Empire in
Paris, France.*

Not long after adopting her new name, Angelou landed a role as the minor character Ruby in a major production of American composer George Gershwin's classic musical, *Porgy and Bess*. The world tour took her to France, Italy, Egypt, Greece, Spain, Morocco,

Switzerland, and other countries. Her mother watched Clyde while she was away. When she returned from her tour, her son informed her that he wanted to change his name as well. From now on, he wanted to be called Guy. She did not object. Family and friends soon got used to the name change.

During her travels, Angelou had begun to develop a new interest: writing. At first she turned out only a few song lyrics and short stories. But what started as an interest quickly became a passion. Before long, she had embarked on a literary adventure that would change her life forever.

In 1957, the newly named Maya Angelou recorded Miss Calypso, *an album of both calypso standards and her own songs. Among the Angelou originals were "Mambo in Africa," "Neighbor, Neighbor," and "Tamo." The record was reissued in 1996 as a CD.*

Chapter

6 JOURNEYS IN AFRICA

ꙮ

When 29-year-old Maya Angelou began dabbling
in writing in 1957, she felt that she should show
someone her work. She realized she needed the
input of an expert who could tell her if she had any
talent. So when she was introduced to John Killens,
she eagerly showed him her initial writings. Killens
was a black fiction writer who belonged to the well-
known Harlem Writers Guild in New York City. This
group consisted of several writers who met on a
regular basis in Killens' home to critique one another's work. Killens told Angelou that she had promise
as a writer. He urged her to come to New York and
join the guild.

Encouraged, Angelou collected Guy and moved
to New York. At first the sharp criticism of the guild

*In her early 30s, Maya Angelou spent a year
living and working in Cairo, Egypt.*

John Killens
(1916–1987)

members made her feel disheartened. But Killens explained that the critical comments would help her reshape her work and improve as a writer. So she stuck with it. Determined to become the best writer she could be, she sang at a local nightclub to pay the bills while she honed her craft.

Her hard work paid off. In 1960, 32-year-old Angelou published a short story in a Cuban magazine, *Revolución*. She was thrilled. She felt that her writing career had truly begun.

Angelou also became involved in the civil rights movement that was steadily taking hold in the United States. Hearing the great civil rights leader Martin Luther King Jr. speak in a Harlem church inspired her. She and some friends decided to put on a show to raise money for King's organization, the Southern Christian Leadership Conference (SCLC). Angelou wrote and produced the performance, which they called "Cabaret for Freedom." The show ran for five weeks to sold-out houses. By all measures, it was a great success.

Members of the SCLC were impressed with Angelou's efforts and commitment to the cause. They offered her the position of Northern coordinator for the SCLC. She spent the next seven months writing letters, managing volunteers, and raising money for the cause of civil rights.

The following year, in 1961, she formed the Cultural Association for Women of African Heritage (CAWAH) with members of the Harlem Writers Guild. The group's mission was to lend support to other

Civil rights activists staged a sit-in to integrate a Nashville, Tennessee, lunch counter in 1961.

The modern civil rights movement began in the 1950s, as African-Americans worked to gain equality with whites. Various groups fought the battle in different ways. While the Southern Christian Leadership Conference and the Cultural Association for Women of African Heritage staged protests and marches to call attention to unfair practices, groups such as the National Association for the Advancement of Colored People used the court system to challenge unjust laws.

civil rights groups by producing theatrical benefits and participating in public protests. But the larger civil rights community viewed the CAWAH as being too radical, and the organization disbanded. But Angelou had become an activist, and soon her attention turned to the struggle in South Africa.

In 1960, Angelou attended a gathering at John Killens' house. Killens had invited a South African freedom fighter named Vusumzi Make to speak at the event. At the time, South Africa had a white-run government that openly practiced racism and oppressed the local black people. Vusumzi—called Vus for short—had come to New York to ask the United Nations to pressure the South African government to change its racist policies.

Angelou was strongly attracted to Make, and the two decided to share an apartment in New York. They made plans to marry, and although they were never officially wed, they considered themselves to be husband and wife.

In 1960, Angelou was offered a role in an off-

Broadway play titled *The Blacks*. The drama, by French playwright Jean Genet, was a controversial political play. Genet suggested that if blacks ran society, they might oppress people in the same way that whites had long oppressed blacks. Angelou's first reaction to reading the play was to reject this idea and refuse to be in the show. But Make convinced her to say yes. He told her:

Actor James Earl Jones performed in a scene from The Blacks *in 1961.*

This play is great. If they still want you,
you must do this play. ... You see, my dear
wife, most black revolutionaries, most
black radicals, most black activists, do not
really want change. They want exchange
[to switch places with white people]. This
play points to that likelihood. And our
people need to face the temptation. You
must act in The Blacks.

Not long after Angelou's debut in *The Blacks*, Vus announced that he wanted to move with Maya and Guy to Egypt. There he planned to meet with freedom fighters from several other African countries. On arriving in Egypt's capital, Cairo, Angelou was captivated by the city's exotic atmosphere. "When we entered the center of Cairo," she later wrote, "the avenues burst wide open with such a force of color, people, action and smells, I was stripped of cool composure."

After living in Cairo for a few months, Angelou found that Make was not making enough money to pay the bills. She decided to get a job. She managed to land the position of associate editor of a local English-language magazine, the *Arab Observer*. She thought Make would be pleased, but he was very upset. He yelled at her for taking a job without getting his permission. Angelou had never considered that she needed a man's permission to work, and she suddenly found herself falling out of love with someone she now realized was sexist and controlling. She later remembered, "The last wisps of mystery had disappeared. There had been physical attraction … [But now] he was just a fat man, standing over me, scolding."

Leaving Make, in 1962 Angelou took Guy and moved to the West African nation of Ghana. Her

Angelou's move to Ghana helped her feel more connected to her African heritage.

main motivation was to enroll her son, now 17, in the widely respected University of Ghana. Soon after they arrived, she found a job as an administrative assistant at the university's School of Music and Drama. She also wrote articles for local newspapers *Ghanaian Times* and *African Review*, and acted in a production of the Bertolt Brecht play *Mother Courage and Her Children*, staged by the univerity's drama department.

Angelou felt at home in Ghana. Of its people, she later wrote:

> *Their skins were the colors of my childhood cravings: peanut butter, licorice, chocolate, and caramel. Theirs was the laughter of home, quick and without artifice [falseness]. The erect and graceful walk of the women reminded me of my Arkansas grandmother. ... So I had finally come home.*

While in Ghana, Angelou felt the urge to learn more about her African roots. She visited the places where Europeans had once bought

---

The nation of Ghana occupies the site of a powerful medieval empire of the same name. The region also witnessed the rise of another strong kingdom—Ashanti—in late medieval times. These empires declined over time. One major reason was the influence of white European slave traders and colonizers. Portuguese merchants set up forts and slave markets on Ghana's coast. And the British turned the area into a colony in the late 1800s. Ghana gained its independence in 1957, shortly before Angelou arrived there. She found a proud people who delighted in controlling their own land and fates.

slaves to carry across the Atlantic. She also spoke with the residents of local villages. These journeys taught her a great deal about the terrible era of the slave trade and made her think about her ancestors. "Not all slaves were stolen," she came to realize, "nor were all slave dealers European." In fact, many black chiefs had sold other blacks to the Europeans. Did the ancestor of one of the villagers, she wondered, sell Angelou's own ancestor? She asked, "Did that

Maya Angelou spent nearly four years in Africa, during which time she learned a number of African languages.

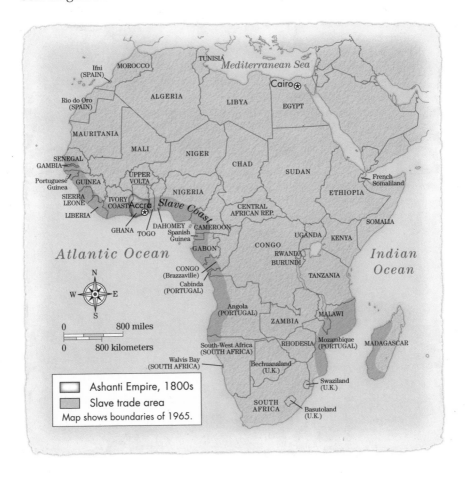

Ashanti Empire, 1800s
Slave trade area
Map shows boundaries of 1965.

grandmother's grandmother grow fat on the sale of my grandmother's grandmother?"

Another important experience Angelou had while in Ghana was getting to know Malcolm X, whom she had met briefly before in New York City. The famous American civil rights activist arrived in Ghana's

Malcolm X advocated armed self-defense for blacks. He hoped to unite African-Americans in their struggle for freedom.

capital, Accra. As she drove him to various meetings and rallies, they became friends.

After he returned to the United States, Malcolm X stayed in touch with Angelou, and he eventually asked her to return as well to run the offices of his Organization of Afro-American Unity. Angelou felt compelled to work for such an important cause. In 1965, she returned to California, feeling that her years in Africa had been highly rewarding. "If the heart of Africa remained elusive," she wrote, "my search for it had brought me closer to understanding myself and other human beings."

While Angelou was in Africa, an important piece of civil rights legislation was signed into law in the United States. The Civil Rights Act of 1964 made racial discrimination illegal in public places, such as theaters and restaurants. It also required employers to offer equal job opportunities to African-Americans and stated that projects involving federal money would lose their funding if there was evidence of discrimination on the job.

7 GROWING ACCLAIM AS A WRITER

❧◦◦◦◦◦

Maya Angelou was 37 when she returned to San Francisco early in 1965. She was looking forward to working with Malcolm X. But this was not to be. Less than two days after she arrived in California, the black nationalist leader was assassinated while addressing a meeting of the Organization of Afro-American Unity.

Three years later, civil rights leader Martin Luther King Jr., whom Angelou knew from her work with the Southern Christian Leadership Conference, was murdered. An Angelou biographer points out:

> *The murders of Malcolm X and Martin Luther King deeply affected Angelou. She had known so many civil rights workers who had been killed or imprisoned. The*

In 1971, 43-year-old Maya Angelou posed with a first edition of her autobiography I Know Why the Caged Bird Sings.

65 ❧◦◦

Martin Luther King Jr. (left) and Malcolm X smiled for photographers during a 1964 encounter at the U.S. Capitol. It was their only meeting.

riots in Los Angeles, Detroit, Baltimore, and elsewhere that erupted after King's death left Angelou grasping with unanswered questions. What would happen to the [civil rights] movement now? What kind of country would do this to its heroes?

Though 1968 had started out on a tragic note with the assassination of Martin Luther King Jr., that year also proved a bright one for Angelou's writing career. She wrote several poems, and she recorded an album—aptly titled *The Poetry of Maya Angelou*—on which she read the poems aloud. She also wrote a 10-part series for National Educational Television. Called *Black, Blues, Black*, it dealt with African traditions still common in American life.

> *Martin Luther King Jr. was assassinated on April 4, 1968. This date also marked Maya Angelou's 40th birthday. Because the date took on an unhappy association after King's death, Angelou refused to celebrate her birthday for many years.*

Thanks to these efforts, Angelou's name was becoming increasingly known in literary and artistic circles. This hit home one day when she was in New York City. She had just been named Person of the Week by a major newspaper, the *New York Post*. When she walked into a bar that she frequented, a crowd gathered around her. Among the admirers and well-wishers were writers, actors, models, musicians, journalists, and college professors.

Important people like these knew other influential people. Such contacts had the potential to help further Angelou's career. This is exactly what happened in the case of the famous African-American author James Baldwin. She and Baldwin had become friends, and one night in 1968, he took her to a dinner party at the home of the well-known cartoonist Jules Feiffer. The partygoers were fascinated as Angelou told them some of the more colorful incidents of her life.

The following day, Feiffer's wife called her friend Robert Loomis, an editor at Random House, one of the world's leading publishers. She told Loomis about Angelou and suggested that he publish Angelou's autobiography. Loomis promptly called Angelou and asked her if she was interested in writing the story of her life. At first she was somewhat reluctant. "I'm pretty certain that I will not write an autobiography," she said. "I have only had my fortieth birthday this year. Maybe in ten or twenty years." They both laughed.

But Loomis did not give up. He called her several more times. Eventually she gave in. "I'll start tomorrow," she finally told him. Titled *I Know Why the Caged Bird Sings*, the book was published in 1970. The title comes from the poem "Sympathy" by the

James Baldwin (1924–1987)

noted black poet Paul Laurence Dunbar. The poem reads in part:

> *I know why the caged bird sings, ah me,*
> *When his wing is bruised and his bosom*
> *   sore,—*
> *When he beats his bars and he would be free;*
> *It is not a carol of joy or glee,*
> *But a prayer that he sends from his heart's*
> *   deep core,*
> *But a plea, that upward to Heaven he flings—*
> *I know why the caged bird sings!*

The book was a frank telling of Angelou's life from her youth in Stamps, Arkansas, to the birth of her son in 1945. In a sense, she had bared her soul to the public, sparing none of the darker and more embarrassing episodes. The poverty and prejudice were there. Even the rape and stabbing she had experienced were included. Those who read the book were moved by how a young woman had overcome so much adversity and made something of her life. The quality

Paul Laurence Dunbar (1872–1906)

Seeing that his friend was reluctant to write down her life story, writer James Baldwin dared Angelou to write her autobiography by telling her it was the most difficult thing a writer could do. Angelou took the challenge, and Baldwin couldn't have been more pleased with the result. He wrote: "This book liberates the reader into life simply because Maya Angelou confronts her own life with such a moving wonder, such a luminous dignity. I have no words for this achievement; but I know that not since the days of my childhood, when the people in books were more real than the people one saw every day, have I found myself so moved. ... Her portrait is a biblical study of life in the midst of death."

of her writing was also apparent to all.

I Know Why the Caged Bird Sings was an instant hit. In one week it made the nonfiction bestseller list. Angelou was the first African-American woman to ever achieve this distinction. The book was also nominated for the much-coveted National Book Award. In addition, many university courses made the title required reading.

Angelou began receiving invitations to speak at colleges and universities across the country. She accepted some of these. For a while, though, she rejected all offers from schools in the American South. According to one of Angelou's biographers, having experienced as a child the deep-seated hatred of blacks by many white people in the region, "[t]he South had become an obsession, a place on which to fasten all her anger and fear about racism."

Eventually, however, Angelou's attitude changed. She came to feel that refusing to deal with her anger about the South was not helpful to her. It would be better, she decided, to face her fears. That might help her to grow as a person.

To that end, Angelou accepted an offer to speak at Wake Forest University in Winston-Salem, North Carolina. She was very nervous about the lecture. She even asked a friend to go with her for support. But her reception there changed everything. She later recalled:

At a speech at the University of Northern Iowa in 2000, Angelou talked about the healing nature of poetry.

I walked to the podium, and looked out into a filled and racially mixed auditorium. … I had never actually imagined whites and blacks sitting together in a Southern state. Understandably, I was taken aback.

Angelou delivered her lecture on African traditions brought to America by slaves, fully expecting a backlash. Again, however, she was surprised. She wrote:

If I was thrown before, now I was dumbfounded. I had pulled no punches, and softened no points, yet Whites stood beside Blacks, clapping their hands and smiling.

While lecturing on the college circuit, Angelou was offered the job of writing a screenplay. Columbia Pictures was planning to make a film based on the book The Autobiography of Malcolm X, *which writer Alex Haley wrote based on conversations with the civil rights activist. Angelou completed the script, but the movie was never made.*

A university official even invited Angelou to teach black literature and history at the university. She had never considered the possibility of teaching and did not accept the job at that time, but she was surprised and flattered by the offer.

Angelou began to realize that she had been mistaken. The South *had* changed. Some bitterness and tensions still existed between the races, but the important initial steps toward a more equal and fair-minded society had been made. This filled her with hope. It would also color the tone of her later writings.

In 1971, Angelou published a volume of poetry titled *Just Give Me a Cool Drink of Water 'Fore I Diiie*. These poems explore the experience of being black and a woman in America. They also speak of

As Angelou became more well-known as an author, she was often asked to give interviews.

experiences, both large and small, that are common to all human beings. A number of poems in this collection examine small facets of the human condition that most people take for granted. For example, "No Loser, No Weeper" deals with the frustration of losing things:

I lost a doll once and cried for a week.
She could open her eyes, and do all but speak.
I believe she was took, by some doll-snatching
*   sneak.*
I tell you, I hate to lose something.

A watch of mine once, got up and walked away.
It had twelve numbers on it and for the time of
*   the day.*
I'll never forget it and all I can say
Is I really hate to lose something.

The book was nominated for the Pulitzer Prize in literature. This is one of the highest awards given to writers.

In addition, Angelou wrote an original screenplay for a movie that was released in 1972. Made by a Swedish filmmaker named Stig Björkman, it was titled *Georgia, Georgia*. The story concerns a young black woman who falls in love with a white man. This was another first for Angelou. No other African-American woman had ever written the script for a feature film that was released to the public. To many,

it seemed as though Maya Angelou had reached the pinnacle of writing success. But they were wrong. Even prouder moments were in her future. ❧

Maya Angelou on the set of Georgia, Georgia with director Stig Björkman

8 A FLURRY OF BOOKS AND AWARDS

❧❦❧

With the large number of writing projects she had tackled, Maya Angelou had kept herself almost constantly busy. In fact, while working she became a sort of hermit. She told her friends not to disturb her, unplugged her phone, and closed her drapes. Then she would write for up to 16 hours a day. Usually the only thing she ate during these bouts of solitude was a little bread and cheese.

Under such conditions, Angelou had little time for personal relationships. That included relationships with men. But when she met Paul Du Feu at a dinner party, she decided he was someone worth making time for. Du Feu was a carpenter, cartoonist, and writer. He was also English, white, and several years younger than she.

Maya Angelou tended to her garden in a 1988 publicity photo.

The two were married in 1973 in a church in San Francisco. She was 45 at the time. Almost immediately, they moved to California's Sonoma Valley, the heart of that state's wine country. There they found an old ranch house on 2 acres (0.8 hectares) of land and remodeled it to suit their tastes. Angelou chose to decorate several of the walls with African masks and sketches of black women and children. She also made time for her child and grandchild. Her son, Guy, now grown, had recently settled in the San Francisco area. He was married and had a son named Colin.

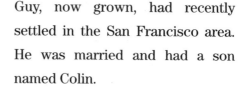

Angelou's son, Guy Johnson, is also a published author. His two novels, Standing at the Scratch Line *and* Echoes of a Distant Summer, *explore the complicated and varied life stories of two generations of African-American men.*

The fact that Du Feu was a writer himself proved beneficial to Angelou. He encouraged her to write. He also urged her to be as frank as she dared in baring herself to her readers. She took this advice in writing her second autobiography, *Gather Together in My Name,* published in 1974. The book chronicles her several years of personal struggle following Guy's birth in the mid-1940s.

It was while she was working on *Gather Together in My Name* that Angelou began a new writing routine that she has followed ever since. It begins at 5:30 in the morning. After showering, she leaves the

house, preferring to write somewhere else. She has described what happens next:

When I'm writing, I keep a hotel room. I have everything taken off the walls, and I bring in yellow pads, a Roget's Thesaurus, a dictionary, a Bible, a deck of cards and a bottle of sherry [red wine]. I sit at a little table and play solitaire. My grandmother used to say when I was young, "You know, that's not even on my littlest mind." And so I determined that the human being has a big mind and a little mind. The cards occupy my little mind so I can get to the big mind and hear the language. ... I can edit at home. I can do that at night, after I've made dinner. ... I'll take the pages of the morning and look at them. If I do five pages in longhand, that's good. If I do seven, hello!

Playing solitaire helps Angelou write by quieting her mind.

This routine proved successful. In the late 1970s, Angelou produced a flurry of books that further expanded her professional reputation. She wrote two more books of poetry—*Oh Pray My Wings Are Gonna Fit Me Well* (1975) and *And Still I Rise* (1978). She also published a third autobiography, titled *Singin' and Swingin' and Gettin' Merry Like Christmas*, in 1976.

In addition, Angelou found time to act again. In 1977, she played Kunta Kinte's grandmother in the renowned TV miniseries based on Alex Haley's novel *Roots*. Haley had dramatized the story of his ancestors' plight. Many had been American slaves descended from Kinte, an African who had been kidnapped into slavery and brought across the Atlantic. Angelou felt a strong connection to the story. She knew that as an African-American, she was descended from slaves as well. She received an Emmy nomination for her powerful performance in *Roots*. Still another

In February 2008, a television program, African American Lives 2, explored Angelou's own African roots. A DNA test showed that her ancestors were members of the Mende people of West Africa. They were kidnapped and brought to North America as slaves. The program also revealed that Angelou's great-grandfather was white. Her great-grandmother had been born a slave named Mary Lee. At age 17, after slavery had been outlawed, she had a child by her former owner, a white man named John Savin. After Savin forced Lee to sign a false statement naming another man as the father, Lee and her child were sent to the poorhouse. The child was Angelou's maternal grandmother, Marguerite Baxter.

Angelou posed with Roots *author Alex Haley (center) and lead actor LeVar Burton.*

honor came when a PBS documentary she wrote—
Afro-Americans in the Arts—won a Golden Eagle
Award. And her first autobiography, *I Know Why*

the Caged Bird Sings, was made into a TV movie in 1977. Although Angelou wrote the screenplay, she was not consulted on many of the artistic decisions. The film brought her story to an even wider audience, but it failed to live up to the book's promise and was a disappointment to her.

These and other projects kept Angelou extremely busy. Her increasing fame demanded even more of her time for interviews and award ceremonies. This eventually put a strain on her marriage. She and Du Feu were a loving couple, she later wrote, "determined to live with flair and laughter." But Du Feu had trouble adjusting to the hectic schedule of a famous wife. They separated in 1981 after eight years of marriage. Angelou recalled:

> *As the fame and the success increased and the books were bestsellers, and I became the first Black producer in Hollywood, he couldn't stand it. ... I brought all my energy and laughter and frivolity and seriousness to the marriage and it failed. It wore out. I don't think I failed. It failed.*

Angelou later reflected on her relationships and marriages:

> *[I]n each marriage I brought all of myself and put in all my energy and*

Angelou enjoys entertaining her friends in her home; cooking is a special skill and source of pleasure.

loyalty, excitement, fidelity and hard work. The only thing is, when a marriage doesn't work I am one to say, "Hey, I'm unhappy, and it's not given to me to live a long time." So I've left a number of men, but I've been loved a great deal and have loved a great deal.

After the breakup with Du Feu, Angelou moved east to Winston-Salem, North Carolina. She had decided to take the teaching position at Wake Forest University that had been offered to her so many years earlier. There she bought a big house with 10 rooms, which she later expanded to 18.

When people asked Angelou if she minded living alone in such a large house, she smiled and said no. She explained that she had given up on finding just the right man to spend the rest of her life with. The main reason was that having a successful marriage requires a lot of time and effort. She would rather devote that time and effort to her professional endeavors.

Though Angelou was no longer interested in marriage, she had not given up on people and friendship. Other close relationships and friendships were developing to enrich her life. Among the more fruitful of these would be one with the famous media personality Oprah Winfrey. ❧

9 FROM HARDSHIP TO TRIUMPH

❧❀❧

Maya Angelou's remarkable string of professional achievements continued into the early 1980s and beyond. Not long after she moved to Winston-Salem to teach at Wake Forest University, the school sweetened the offer. She was named Reynolds Professor of American Studies and given a lifetime appointment, an honor given to few in the academic world. Many observers commented that this was an amazing feat for a woman who had never attended college herself.

Angelou also continued to turn out popular, successful books and other literary works. Her fourth autobiography, *The Heart of a Woman*, appeared in 1981. Another volume of poetry, *Shaker, Why Don't You Sing*, was published two years later. In

For her many inspiring and accessible poems, as well as for her many public presentations, Maya Angelou has become known as the "people's poet."

> *Although Angelou never attended college herself, she has been awarded more than 30 honorary doctorates from various universities. She is very proud of these degrees and prefers to be called "Dr. Angelou."*

1985, she wrote a play titled *The Southern Journey*. A fifth autobiography, *All God's Children Need Traveling Shoes*, and still another poetry book, *Now Sheba Sings the Song*, followed in 1986 and 1987, respectively.

Based partly on her impressive literary output, North Carolina's governor appointed Angelou to the state's arts council. This seemed fitting. Many critics and writers were hailing her as a Renaissance woman for her accomplishments as a poet, playwright, actress, and public speaker.

In 1993, Angelou read her poem "On the Pulse of Morning" at the inauguration of President Bill Clinton. Her performance became a kind of electric spark that ignited a new burst of popularity. Hardcover sales of her first autobiography, *I Know Why the Caged Bird Sings*, rose by an incredible 1,500 percent. Offers poured in for her to speak at colleges and town halls. The following year she won a Grammy award for an album in which she read "On the Pulse of Morning."

In 1993, Angelou published a book of essays titled *Wouldn't Take Nothing for My Journey Now*. She dedicated it to the famous talk-show host, actor, and humanitarian Oprah Winfrey.

Angelou and Winfrey met nearly a decade before

Maya Angelou accepted her award for Best Spoken Word Album at the 36th annual Grammy Awards in 1994.

when Winfrey, a young reporter, interviewed Angelou. Over the years the women developed a strong friendship. Today Winfrey considers Angelou to be her mentor, and she describes the older woman's special qualities in this way:

> *In all the days of my life, I never met a woman who was more completely herself than Maya Angelou. ... When you walk into a room and she's there, you know it. She is fully aware of what it means to be human, and share that humanity with others. Being around her makes you want to do the same, be more fully your own self.*

In 2000, Maya Angelou was awarded the National Medal of Arts by President Bill Clinton. This is the highest award given to artists by the U.S. government. The award is given to individuals or groups who are "deserving of special recognition by reason of their outstanding contributions to the excellence, growth, support and availability of the arts in the United States."

Angelou's many appearances on Winfrey's talk show, *The Oprah Winfrey Show*, brought her greater attention and a wider audience. Winfrey also threw enormous birthday parties for her mentor. These took place in 1993, when Angelou was 65, in 1998, when she was 70, and 2003, when she was 75. Each event was attended by hundreds of Hollywood and literary celebrities.

Over the past two decades, Angelou has continued to write for film and television—as well as acting in those media. In 1993, she wrote the poetry used in the movie *Poetic Justice*, a film about

an African-American poet. She also acted in that movie, as well as in the 1995 feature *How to Make an American Quilt* and 2006's *Madea's Family Reunion*, among others. She has also tried her hand at directing with the 1998 movie *Down in the Delta*, which chronicles the contemporary and historical troubles of an African-American family. With the help of Oprah Winfrey, she has also branched off into

Oprah Winfrey and her mentor appeared together at a leadership conference in 2001.

91 ✺

Angelou appears with castmates in the 2006 movie Madea's Family Reunion.

radio. In 2006, Angelou became a radio talk show host for the first time, hosting a weekly show for XM Satellite Radio's "Oprah & Friends" channel.

Of course Angelou has continued to write poems and books and give lectures and speeches. She wrote two books of poetry for children, *Soul Looks Back in Wonder* and *My Painted House, My Friendly Chicken, and Me.* She published a cookbook that in typical Angelou fashion marries recipes and recollections. She has also worked with Hallmark to launch a collection of greeting cards, Maya Angelou's

Life Mosaic. She explained:

For many years, Hallmark asked me to do it, but I said no. Then I met the Hallmark people, and I liked them. I spoke to a person who figures heavily in my life and said, "I'm thinking of doing some work for Hallmark." He said, "You can't do that—you're the people's poet." After I got off the phone, I said, "Wait a minute—if I'm the people's poet, shouldn't I write for the people? There are people who never read a book, but I can get an idea over to them on a greeting card."

Now in her eighth decade, Maya Angelou continues to learn, grow, and create. But she complains about getting older: "What's really hard ... is not the thickening of the waist or the cracking of the hips and knees. It's the absence of the beloveds. Some people who start with you go on before you to their other destinations."

Angelou has a rich life to look back on, but she continues to look forward. Her lifelong study of the human condition has given her a deep respect for

In her cookbook, titled Hallelujah! The Welcome Table, *Maya Angelou shares her favorite recipes and related stories from her rich and varied life. In one of the stories, Angelou recounts the difficulty she had finding work after returning to the United States from Africa in the mid-1960s. But after cooking a traditional Southern breakfast for a homesick business owner, Angelou was offered a job as a writer for a publicity agency. The owner told her, "You can start on Monday. ... [I]f you can write half as good as you can cook, you are going to be famous."*

Angelou appeared with her son, Guy (left), and grandson, Colin (right), and their wives and children in a 2005 holiday television program.

humanity and taught her to admire people from all walks of life. Almost everyone she meets feels similar respect and admiration for her. To them, she is an example of a person who has gone from the depths to the heights. Utilizing some remarkable strengths and talents, she has risen from poverty, ignorance, and hardship to personal triumph, wisdom, and worldwide fame. According to Angelou, the trick is never to give up. She says:

In all my work, I try to say you may enounter many defeats, but you must not be defeated. So, if I'm able to say, here we are, human being, we stumble, we fumble and we fall, and then, amazingly, we rise—amazingly! From pain and fear and embarrassment and loss ... and yet some-how we do. ... That's amazing!

Her poem "Still I Rise" sums up the wonder of her life's achievement:

Just like moons and like suns
With the certainty of tides,
Just like hopes springing high,
Still I'll rise. ❧

ANGELOU'S LIFE

1928

Born Marguerite Johnson April 4 in St. Louis, Missouri

1931

Sent by parents to live with her grandmother in Stamps, Arkansas

1940

Graduates from grammar school and moves to San Francisco, California

1940

1929

The U.S. stock market crashes, and severe worldwide economic depression sets in

1936

African-American athlete Jesse Owens wins four gold medals at the Olympic Games in Berlin in the face of Nazi racial discrimination

1941

Japanese bombers attack Pearl Harbor, Hawaii, on December 7, and the United States enters World War II

WORLD EVENTS

1944

Gets a job as a
conductor on
San Francisco's
trolley cars

1945

Gives birth to
a son, Clyde
(later called Guy);
graduates from
high school

1950

Marries
Tosh Angelos

1945

1944

Operation Overlord
begins on D-Day with
the landing of 155,000
Allied troops on the
beaches of Normandy,
France; it is the largest
amphibious military
operation in history

1945

World War II
(1939–1945) ends

1949

Birth of the
People's Republic
of China

ANGELOU'S LIFE

1953

Performs in nightclubs in New York and other cities

1954–1955

Takes part in a world tour of the musical *Porgy and Bess*

1957

Begins writing poetry

1955

1953

Sir Edmund Hillary of New Zealand and Tenzing Norgay of Nepal are the first two men to reach the summit of Mount Everest

1954

In *Brown v. Board of Education*, the Supreme Court rules that deliberate public school segregation is illegal

1957

The Soviet Union launches *Sputnik 1*, the first artificial satellite to orbit Earth; *Sputnik 2*, launched later in the year, carries the first space traveler, a dog named Laika

WORLD EVENTS

1962

Moves to Africa

1970

Publishes her first autobiography, *I Know Why the Caged Bird Sings*

1961

Appears in the off-Broadway play *The Blacks*

1970

1961

A fortified wall is built in Berlin, dividing East and West Germany

1962

Pope John XXIII calls the Second Vatican Council, modernizing Roman Catholicism

1968

Civil rights leader Martin Luther King Jr. and presidential candidate Robert F. Kennedy are assassinated two months apart

ANGELOU'S LIFE

1977

Appears in the TV
miniseries *Roots*,
for which she
receives an Emmy
nomination

1973

Marries writer Paul
Du Feu and moves
to California's
Sonoma Valley

1981

Publishes her fourth
autobiography, *The
Heart of a Woman;*
accepts a teaching
position at Wake
Forest University

1975

1975

Bill Gates and Paul
Allen found Microsoft,
which will become
the world's largest
software company

1980

The United States
boycotts the Olympic
Games in Moscow in
protest of the Soviet
invasion of Afghanistan

1981

Sandra Day O'Connor
becomes the first
woman on the U.S.
Supreme Court

WORLD EVENTS

2000

Awarded the
National Medal
of Arts

1994

Publishes
*The Complete
Collected Poems
of Maya Angelou*

2008

Continues to
give lectures
and readings
throughout
the country

2005

2001

September 11
terrorist attacks on
two World Trade
Center towers in
New York City and
on the Pentagon in
Washington, D.C.,
leave thousands dead

1998

Terrorist bombings
of U.S. embassies
in Tanzania and
Kenya kill 224
people and injure
more than 4,500

2008

Global credit crisis
shakes the world's
economy

DATE OF BIRTH: April 4, 1928

PLACE OF BIRTH: St. Louis, Missouri

FATHER: Bailey Johnson

MOTHER: Vivian Baxter Johnson

EDUCATION: Mission Hills High School, San Francisco, California

CHILDREN: Clyde (Guy) Johnson (1945–)

FIRST SPOUSE: Tosh Angelos

DATE OF MARRIAGE: 1950

SECOND SPOUSE: Paul Du Feu

DATE OF MARRIAGE: 1973

FURTHER READING

Agins, Donna Brown. *Maya Angelou: "Diversity Makes a Rich Tapestry."* Berkeley Heights, N.J.: Enslow Publishers, 2006.

Angelou, Maya. *Poetry for Young People.* Ed. Edwin Graves Wilson. New York: Sterling, 2007.

Angelou, Maya. *Phenomenal Woman.* Ed. Linda Sunshine. New York: Random House, 2000.

Kite, L. Patricia. *Maya Angelou.* Minneapolis: Lerner Publications, 2006.

Spain, Valerie. *Meet Maya Angelou.* New York: Random House, 2003.

LOOK FOR MORE SIGNATURE LIVES
BOOKS ABOUT THIS ERA:

George Washington Carver: *Scientist, Inventor, and Teacher*

Langston Hughes: *The Voice of Harlem*

Percy Lavon Julian: *Pioneering Chemist*

Wilma Mankiller: *Chief of the Cherokee Nation*

Thurgood Marshall: *Civil Rights Lawyer and Supreme Court Justice*

Gloria Steinem: *Champion of Women's Rights*

Amy Tan: *Author and Storyteller*

Nikola Tesla: *Physicist, Inventor, Electrical Engineer*

Alice Walker: *Author and Social Activist*

Booker T. Washington: *Innovative Educator*

ON THE WEB

For more information on this topic,
use FactHound.
1. Go to *www.facthound.com*
2. Choose your grade level.
3. Begin your search.
The book's ID number is 9780756518899
FactHound will find the best
sites for you.

HISTORIC SITES

DuSable Museum of
African-American History
740 E. 56th Place
Chicago, IL 60637
773/947-0600
Exhibits on the historical experiences and
achievements of African-Americans

National Civil Rights Museum
450 Mulberry St.
Memphis, TN 38103
901/521-9699
Museum converted from the motel where
Martin Luther King Jr. was killed; contains
exhibits on the key people and events of
the civil rights movement

assassination
the murder of someone who is well known or important, often for political reasons

calypso
type of music from the West Indies with a lively rhythm and beat

civil rights
person's rights that are guaranteed by the U.S. Constitution

communist
supporter of an economic system in which property is owned by the government or community and profits are shared; personal freedoms are often limited

inauguration
ceremony at which a president is sworn into office

mentor
adviser or teacher

mute
being silent or without speech

radical
favoring extreme changes or reforms

Renaissance woman
woman who has wide interests and is expert in several areas

revolutionaries
people who want to bring about major changes to their government

segregated
when people of different races are kept separate from each other

Chapter 1

Page 9, line 9: Cyndy Dyson. "Biography of Maya Angelou." *Maya Angelou.* Ed. Harold Bloom. Philadelphia: Chelsea House, 2002, p. 43.

Page 10, line 12: Maya Angelou. "On the Pulse of Morning." *The Complete Collected Poems of Maya Angelou.* New York: Random House, 1994, pp. 272–273.

Chapter 2

Page 16, line 19: Maya Angelou. *I Know Why the Caged Bird Sings.* New York: Random House, 1970, p. 5.

Page 16, sidebar: Ibid.

Page 18, line 24: Ibid., p. 25.

Page 19, line 9: Ibid., p. 52.

Page 20, line 22: Ibid., pp. 59–60.

Chapter 3

Page 26, line 4: Ibid., p. 87.

Page 27, lines 12 and 21: Ibid., p. 98.

Page 27, sidebar: Ibid., pp. 99–100.

Page 30, line 19: Ibid., pp. 218–219.

Page 32, lines 6 and 9: Ibid., pp. 245–246.

Chapter 4

Page 36, line 1: Ibid., p. 255.

Page 36, lines 20 and 27: Ibid., p. 266.

Page 37, line 7: Ibid., p. 271.

Page 38, line 7: Ibid., p. 275.

Page 38, line 12: Ibid., p. 281.

Page 38, line 24: Ibid., pp. 285–286.

Page 39, line 17: Ibid.

Chapter 5

Page 44, line 1: Maya Angelou. *Gather Together in My Name.* New York: Random House, 1974, p. 91.

Page 44, lines 12 and 15: Ibid., p. 93.

Page 44, line 28: Ibid., p. 103.

Page 46, line 16: Ibid., p. 122.

Chapter 6

Page 58, line 1: Maya Angelou. *The Heart of a Woman.* New York: Random House, 1981, p. 207.

Page 58, line 16: Ibid., p. 212.

Page 59, line 2: Ibid., p. 227.

Page 60, line 15: Marcia Ann Gillespie, Rosa Johnson Butler, and Richard A. Long. *Maya Angelou: A Glorious Celebration.* New York: Doubleday, 2008, pp. 75–76.

Page 61, lines 5 and 9: "Biography of Maya Angelou," p. 31.

Page 63, line 14: Maya Angelou. *All God's Children Need Traveling Shoes.* New York: Random House, 1986, p. 196.

Chapter 7

Page 65, line 12: "Biography of Maya Angelou," p. 32.

Page 68, line 20: Maya Angelou. *A Song Flung Up to Heaven.* New York: Random House, 2002, p. 207.

Page 68, line 25: Ibid., p. 209.

Page 69, line 3: Paul Laurence Dunbar. "Sympathy." *Paul Laurence Dunbar.* 20 Oct. 2008. www.paullaurencedunbar.net/sympathy.html

Page 70, line 23: "Biography of Maya Angelou," p. 34.

Page 70, sidebar: *Parent Information Center.* 20 Oct. 2008. www.wpic.org/Library/Synoposis/Synopsis_1Page19.html

Page 72, lines 1 and 10: Ibid.

Page 74, line 7: "No Loser, No Weeper." *The Complete Collected Poems of Maya Angelou,* p. 12.

Chapter 8

Page 79, line 3: Teresa K. Weaver. "Maya Angelou's Final Chapter." *Race Matters.* 5 May 2002. 20 Oct. 2008. www.racematters.org/mayaangeloufinal-chapter.htm

Page 83, line 11: "Biography of Maya Angelou," p. 39.

Page 83, line 16: *Maya Angelou: A Glorious Celebration,* p. 120.

Page 83, line 25: "Biography of Maya Angelou," p. 40.

Chapter 9

Page 90, line 3: Oprah Winfrey. "Foreward." *Maya Angelou: A Glorious Celebration,* p. 1.

Page 90, sidebar: *Lifetime Honors: National Medal of Arts.* 20 Oct. 2008. www.nea.gov/honors/medals

Page 93, line 2: *Maya Angelou: A Glorious Celebration,* p. 176.

Page 93, line 21: Dana Kennedy. "Holiday Films: A Poet at 70 Ventures Into the Unknown. *The New York Times.* 15 Nov. 1998.

Page 93, sidebar: Maya Angelou. *Hallelujah! The Welcome Table.* New York: Random House, 2004, p. 137.

Page 95, line 1: Tony Kahn. "On the Bus With Maya Angelou." *Savvy Traveler.* 12 April 2002. 20 Oct. 2008. http://savvytraveler.publicradio.org/show/features/2002/20020412/postcard2.shtml

Page 95, line 11: "Still I Rise." *The Complete Collected Poems of Maya Angelou,* p. 33.

Select Bibliography

Academy of Achievement. "Maya Angelou: America's Renaissance Woman." www.achievement.org/autodoc/page/ang0bio-1

Angelou, Maya. *All God's Children Need Traveling Shoes*. New York: Random House, 1986.

Angelou, Maya. *The Complete Collected Poems of Maya Angelou*. New York: Random House, 1994.

Angelou, Maya. *Gather Together in My Name*. New York: Random House, 1974.

Angelou, Maya. *The Heart of a Woman*. New York: Random House, 1981.

Angelou, Maya. *I Know Why the Caged Bird Sings*. New York: Random House, 1970.

Angelou, Maya. *Singin' and Swingin' and Gettin' Merry Like Christmas*. New York: Random House, 1976.

Angelou, Maya. *A Song Flung Up to Heaven*. New York: Random House, 2002.

Bloom, Harold, ed. *Maya Angelou*. Philadelphia: Chelsea House Publishers, 2002.

Elliot, Jeffrey M. *Conversations With Maya Angelou*. Jackson: University Press of Mississippi, 1989.

Gillespie, Marcia Ann, Rosa Johnson Butler, and Richard A. Long. *Maya Angelou: A Glorious Celebration*. New York: Doubleday, 2008.

Lupton, Mary Jane. *Maya Angelou: A Critical Companion*. Westport, Conn.: Greenwood Press, 1998.

Poetry Credits

In addition to his acclaimed volumes on ancient civilizations, historian Don Nardo has published several biographies of great writers or literary studies of their works. Nardo lives with his wife, Christine, in Massachusetts.

Image Credits